Hardy Holzman Pfeiffer

Hardy Holzman Pfeiffer

BY MICHAEL SORKIN

PHOTOGRAPHS BY NORMAN McGRATH

MONOGRAPHS ON CONTEMPORARY ARCHITECTURE

WHITNEY LIBRARY OF DESIGN, an imprint of Watson-Guptill Publications/New York

GRANADA London Toronto Sydney New York

First published 1981 in New York by Whitney Library of Design,
an imprint of Watson-Guptill Publications,
a division of Billboard Publications, Inc.,
1515 Broadway, New York, N.Y. 10036

Library of Congress Cataloging in Publication Data
Sorkin, Michael.
   Hardy Holzman Pfeiffer.
   (Monographs on contemporary architecture)
   1. Hardy Holzman Pfeiffer Associates.   2. Architec-
ture, Modern — 20th century — United States.   I. Title.
II. Series.
NA737.H29S65   720'.92'2   80-28848
ISBN 0-8230-7264-9

First published in Great Britain 1981 by Granada Publishing
Granada Publishing Limited — Technical Books Division
Frogmore, St Albans, Herts AL2 2NF
and
3 Upper James Street, London W1R 4BP
117 York Street, Sydney, NSW 2000, Australia
100 Skyway Avenue, Rexdale, Ontario M9W 3A6, Canada
61 Beach Road, Auckland, New Zealand
ISBN 0 246 11594 7
Granada®
Granada Publishing®

Manufactured in U.S.A.

First Printing, 1981

Edited by Sharon Lee Ryder and Susan Davis
Designed by Robert Fillie
Set in 11 point Spartan Light

To my parents.

Contents

ACKNOWLEDGMENTS

To Hugh Hardy, Malcolm Holzman, and Norman Pfeiffer for their complete and generous cooperation. To Kathleen "Mike" Thompson of HHPA for her heroic and cheerful assistance organizing the photographs. To Norman McGrath whose excellent photographs are the core of this book. To Susan Davis for shepherding the manuscript through production. And especially to Sharon Lee Ryder, whose series this is, for being the best editor a boy could have.

This Side of Paradigms

"You can do architecture with anything," Hugh Hardy remarked recently with characteristic pith. This is an apt credo for the remarkable body of work the office of Hugh Hardy, Malcolm Holzman, and Norman Pfeiffer has produced over the last fifteen or so years. Natural eclectics, they have done buildings which show such a welter of influences and such sheer inventiveness, as to be nearly beyond classification. Indeed, this resistance to taxonomy is partly deliberate: they have trod a path among the warring camps that have sprung up among the ruins of the broken hegemony of orthodox modernism, cagily refusing to participate in the spate of polemic about architecture's future, preferring simply to make it. As Norman Pfeiffer says, "We'll do almost anything to get a building built."

Hardy Holzman Pfeiffer Associates (HHPA) has probably been most commonly identified with a series of projects in which dramatic results were achieved with minimal means. These are striking for their frank — even garish — celebration of ducts and joists exposed and of off-the-shelf industrial parts and for a spirit of assemblage that seems almost ad hoc, a spirit which directly confronts a functionalist tradition grown gray and rigid. Hardy again: "Architecture was stultifying because there was a way you did it. We wanted to make it different. We said, 'Why can't you make it out of this?'" HHPA's approach was genuinely new, not simply "functionalism in drag," as one critic had it, but a real address to the phony "form follows function" formula that had done so much to diminish architecture. What HHPA did was simply to begin — along with other architects in the midsixties — to look at functional elements formally, to "defunctionalize" them by considering them as objects rather than as sentiments.

This was initially as controversial as it was overdue. HHPA and their kith breathed new life into a modernist imagery that had become so encrusted with negative meanings that many architects were led to repudiate it entirely. Function is a very narrow ground for art to stand on. At its center is a kind of vulgar Platonist error, a misplaced and sinister idealism. What it suggests is that there is a perfectability of building types that can be achieved if form can be reduced to a role of subservience. In addition, it implies that once achieved, this perfection is infinitely replicable. Practically, this conceit has led to an architecture of the arid — visible in the Radiant Cities of urban renewal and in endless cookie-cutter suburbs where order substitutes for harmony. When the pursuit of perfection in the sphere of art cannot confine itself to the single object of its contemplation but seeks to be universal, it is time to write the phenomenon off as art.

HHPA helped pare the functionalist vocabulary of both its mechanistic and its idealistic meanings, leaving the forms themselves bare and useful. HHPA is scarcely the first to be riveted by the beauty of industrial forms, elements that have fascinated and provoked designers for 200 years. What HHPA has done is use them in a frankly decorative way, isolating them not simply from the albatross of modernist rhetoric, but often from their actual uses as well. Is the fan shape above the door at the Best Products Corporate Headquarters a diffuser or a transom? Is the ascending blue tube at the Madison Civic Center a column, a piece of sculpture, part of the air conditioning? Distinctively, in the work of Hardy Holzman Pfeiffer, answers to questions like these don't really matter: the intent is to embellish, not to rationalize.

"We began using inexpensive materials," says Malcolm Holzman, "because that's what our clients could afford." While true, such dissembling remarks mislead. The thrust of HHPA's exploration of budget materials has been to use them against the grain of their cheapness, to direct attention away from their "true" character. Unlike the approach of an architect like Frank Gehry whose use of exposed wood studs, plywood, and corrugated metal aims at asserting the hidden beauty of the ordinary, HHPA's method shoots directly for transcendence. Theirs is not the attitude of "let us find beauty in these humble things," rather "let us find beauty *despite* these humble things." HHPA designs away from the crummy qualities of materials, aiming for alchemy rather than "honesty." The ethic of craft is very strong: details give the appearance of precision and deliberation, not accident or funk. In the lobby of the Minneapolis Orchestra Hall, for example, the "industrial" materials are used to convey an atmosphere of formality and order, as if it were constructed of more conventionally lavish materials, aiming at an equivalent grandeur, if with unfamiliar parts. In a certain way, this is playing safe. Gehry takes greater risks and makes a more compelling point. But by using even cheaper materials than HHPA, he overbegs the question — you really have to strain to make chain link look good.

Hardy Holzman Pfeiffer moves in a new functionalist tradition: functionalism with a human face. The sources for this composite tradition are varied and spring from a new exploration of the constructed landscape, a landscape vastly changed since modern architects first discovered industrial shapes. The modern movement's aesthetic was inspired by forms that flourished in the 19th century, by a tradition that had as its apotheosis the entry of the Great White Fleet into Manila. Echoing Corb's frightful dictum, "a house is a machine for living," the functionalist first wave analogized architecture as machinery, with predictably sordid results. The new wave of the sixties, especially in England and Japan, introduced an updated "postindustrial" imagery, freed of the philosophical chaff that so distorted the legacy of the first functionalists. The amazing series of images promulgated by the likes of Archigram in England and the Metabolists in Japan had a strong impact on newly formed Hardy Holzman Pfeiffer Associates, an affinity visible both in the buildings and in the distinctive black and white, ink, zip, and collage graphics with their striking resemblance to the Archigram/Architectural Association style of the sixties.

THEATER FUNCTIONALISM

But there is another strain in HHPA's neofunctionalist work. Before striking out on his own, Hardy worked for a space of years in the office of theatrical designer Jo Mielziner. The impact of the theater is clear throughout HHPA's work. The twin theatrical movements of the modern era — naturalism and experimentalism — have had a strong effect on theatrical form, breaking down the traditional static relationship between performers and audience across the proscenium. This had led, in theatrical design, to a greater candor about the apparatus of stagecraft, about revealing the means of the theatrical artifice. In conventional theaters there is often a discrepancy between the frank, functionalist character of backstage areas and the decorated auditoriums beyond the footlights. The irony of theater functionalism, however, is that it is functionalism in the service of illusion, meant to draw attention away from itself, to conjure worlds elsewhere. But the welter of flies, pulleys, lights, winches, and turntables has a powerful visual character of its own, and the beauties of this assemblage have not been lost on HHPA.

The theatrical element in Hardy Holzman Pfeiffer's work entails, at the most literal level, an affinity for the visual vocabulary of theatrical apparatus. In the Robert S. Marx and Olmsted theaters, there is a consistency of feeling which suggests that both sides of the fourth wall were cut from the same cloth. This feeling extends from backstage through the auditorium and out into the public areas. However, HHPA's theatricality is not simply involved with mining the rich lode of theater functionalism; there is also an acute awareness of what can be accomplished through the *means* of stagecraft, which is, after all, architecture at its most distilled. At the core of this awareness is an elegant and succinct use of light and lighting at all scales. The Dobell House in Ottawa, Ontario, is a virtual essay in modulated light; the renovation of the St. Louis Art Museum is a complex, sophisticated, purposeful study in the illumination of both spaces and objects; the Denver hall features such subtle refinements as a double stripe of gold leaf applied to undulating balcony fascias, which sparkles in the dimming light, describing the perimeter of the performing area.

Finally, this theatricality induces a strong scenographic sensibility. HHPA's work abounds in tableaux, of little scenes linked architecturally. Their affinity for strong routes of circulation that progress from event to event suggests a kind of theater in which the scenes are changed by the movement of the observer. The routes at the Mt. Healthy School, the Best Products Corporate Headquarters, and Artpark are probably the strongest instances of this effect. At Best it is orchestrated by a passage through framed openings from one set to the next, while at Mt. Healthy space opens and contracts around an unobstructed route in deliberate sequence. Artpark is the most explicit stage set, the separate elements scenographically dispersed out of doors against a backdrop of river and trees. In these projects, references are more fantasy than scholarship, sources of dream worlds like stage sets. Best carries a motif of references to high architecture, Artpark to "native" building.

NATIVE FUNCTIONALISM

There is still another strand in the kind of composite functionalism that informs so much of HHPA's work—a feeling for what might, for want of a better description, be called "native" functionalism. Not the studied, crisp aesthetic of the international style with all its orthogonality and thinness, its obsession with planes, this functionalism celebrates the aesthetic of the practical, the tinker's aesthetic, elegant in the scientific sense. Hardy Holzman Pfeiffer is strongly attracted to the artfully wrought conveniences of the American landscape—to silos, oil tanks, Butler buildings, and trussed highway signs. These are the direct equivalent in the landscape of the ducts, joists, bolted joinery, and curtain wall that make up the bits of individual buildings. Both sets of elements are distinguished, on the one hand, by their high degree of technical refinement and, on the other, by their dumbness. While the inherent beauties— both functionally and formally—of these elements are readily accessible, the means by which they may be incorporated into "serious" architecture remain always to be invented. Several stylistic syntheses have lately emerged and among them HHPA's is one of the most successful.

The familiar rubric, "high tech," has been invoked by many to describe this synthesis. High tech has two poles in its current manifestation. One of these has to do with the discovery by the New York decorator crowd of the hardware and restaurant supply stores on Canal Street, the southern boundary of Soho. The other is the actual legacy of functionalism, whether in its Richard Meier or Richard Rogers incarnation. What unites the two groups is a feeling for machined forms and a strong spirit of rectitude in their use. While HHPA clearly admires this set of formal sources, what makes them different is that instead of rectitude there is a sense of play and a love of apparent accident. Simplicity and formal coherence are not mainstays of the HHPA palette; instead there is richness and ambiguity.

THE TRADITION OF THE OLD

A collective imagination as active as HHPA's naturally ranges for sources far beyond the imagery of functionalism, no matter how broadly defined. In this search they are not alone. The problem, as ever, is one of integration. The major current tendency seeking to cook raw elements of the built landscape into an architectural stew is so-called postmodernism. While postmodernism began life as an attitude, it has by now attained the trappings of a style. No longer the expression of a sort of visual pluralism, it has come to have a series of recognizable characteristics and conventions about such matters as the color and coursing of brick, about simple, punctured windows, about minimum composition, about deliberate banality, about historicism, and about what degree of freedom of juxtaposition and combination is to be indulged. The bottom line in the current postmodernist *schtick* is to paste an Adamesque moulding onto an essentially Corbusian interior, a mainly literary operation and a foolish one.

This literary failing has to do with an overreverence toward architectural tradition. The literary champ of postmodernism is T.S. Eliot, whose view of tradition was of "something to be obtained by great labor," something which was to be worshiped and stuck to. The solemnity implicit in this view—as expressed by critics like Eliot and F.R. Leavis—leads to two difficulties. First is the feeling that all work must be expressive of its traditional wellsprings (and that it must have them consciously). Second, and perhaps more discouraging, is the notion that the tastes and predilictions expressed in a building must somehow be validated by being incorporated into a canon. What this means is that an interesting observation—about the consumer landscape by the highway, for example—is distorted by the insistence that its inclusion in a project is tantamount to the invention of art. This is the same operation that makes pop art, a scintillating and compelling observation, into "high art," which it is not. That a Jasper Johns should sell for more than a Rembrandt is absurd on the face of it.

A more useful attitude toward tradition is that taken by Ezra Pound, who described it as "a beauty which we preserve and not a set of fetters to bind us," an attitude which seems more in line with the spirit embodied in HHPA's work. After all, a duct is a duct and a Butler building is neither a primitive hut nor a Doric temple. HHPA can jumble allusions with conviction because they are so frank about it. When they have used off-the-shelf buildings, they have—as at Shaw University—used them straight, representing them as only a little more than what they are, with no self-congratulatory Greek columns necessary. Because they are comfortable with the elements of a variety of traditions, they are able to operate comfortably within them in a way which many architects are not. This extends well beyond the wholesale inclusion of various architectural *objets trouvés* in their work. In the scheme for an addition to the Willard Hotel in Washington, D.C.—a prominently sited, Beaux-Arts pile designed by Henry Hardenburgh, architect of such treasures as the Plaza Hotel and the Dakota Apartments in New York City— HHPA unabashedly decks the scheme out in the same vocabulary as the original but taken a little less seriously. While the addition is not particularly Beaux-Arts in plan and massing, it moves absolutely in the spirit of the Willard without parodying it, patronizing it, or failing it. HHPA has come up with the style for the job, yet without proffering solemnities about its larger meanings. Like a stage set, it recreates the original's feeling without reproducing it.

THE ECLECTIC CIRCUS

There is a name for this attitude, and it is "eclecticism," a concept that has only recently returned to a measure of repute. Meaningful eclecticism must struggle to transcend pastiche, to reveal not simply an attitude but a full measure of architectural substance. Tafuri is succinct on this problem, distinguishing between "Romantic" eclecticism and an eclecticism allied to "new technology," which he describes as the "only possible and legitimate way out" of "the impossible fusion of a present that is feared in the very moment in which one takes stable roots in it, and a past that one refuses to read as such, whose sense one is frightened of: because an exact reading of the past would necessarily lead to the discovery of the sense of *the today* that the Romantic eclectic artist tries desperately not to see." A growing repudiation of the tradition of the new was particularly striking in the American seventies, which gestated a generation not simply of antimodernists (in the broad sense of modern) but of out-and-out revivalists. Hardy Holzman Pfeiffer is among a small group of architects who attempt a serious synthesis of the technology that has increasing resonances in architectural practice and a broader sense of architecture's historical meanings, supporting a usefully inexact reading of the past.

DECRIMINALIZING ORNAMENT

Informed by this sense of combination, HHPA's work has in recent years achieved a new maturity, and with it has come a sense of greater relaxation, a sloughing off of the restless and occasionally overbearing energy of some of the early work. Much of this seems to stem from taking a wider historical view, perhaps the result of their long and meticulous work recycling older buildings and studying their ornament and details. John Ruskin, that font of architectural aphorism, wrote in *Seven Lamps of Architecture*, "I believe the right question to ask respecting all ornament is simply this: was it done with enjoyment—was the carver happy while he was about it." This generous misperception speaks to a discovery that may also have contributed to a certain shift in HHPA's work: that the possibilities of certain systems of inventing ornament are limited. Such is surely the case with their early decorative functionalist buildings: wonderful stuff while it's fresh but easily learned and easily exhausted. The problem is that these "high-tech" materials have too great a uniformity of texture and grain. Trying to defy this formal austerity by whimsical or irregular applications is ultimately frustrating: the irregular use of regular materials always recalls the material's regularity.

THE STYLE FOR CERTAIN JOBS

HHPA's composite functionalist work has, in general, whatever its abstract compositional qualities, benefited as architecture from programs to which it seems especially suited. The Spartan, utilitarian look of the Firemen's Training Center, for instance, its main building bermed like a bunker and sited like a hangar along a runway, is certainly "expressive" of the paramilitary quality of what goes on within. The steel pillboxes which peep out over the roof speak similarly of the real danger of the induced conflagrations produced across the tarmac to train the neophyte fire fighters. The buildings designed for children profit for a different set of reasons. As anyone who remembers childhood will attest, order is not the child's benchmark. Childhood is that time of life when we are freest, most open to explorations of all kinds, when free association, word games, and nonsense are as possible and as plausible as the more rigorous thinking into which adulthood straightjackets us. No child would have thought of functionalism. Yet, HHPA's open plan schools have a kind of complexity that is accessible to children, not the kind of forced complexity that results from the rigorous application of some semimathematical theory, but the accidental, serendipitous complexity of Alice in Wonderland— whatever secret chess games lurk underneath. No matter how artfully contrived, the leftover spaces seem to be casual and happy. HHPA's schools, children's museums, and exhibit work are schematic in structure and organization, concealing no deep meanings, making instead a certain number of simple points about building structure and function apparent, even to little eyes. Taken as a group, the work for children is probably the firm's most uninhibited and successful.

THE OTHER SIDE OF DISCRETE

If this sensibility were reduced to a single attribute, it would be a fascination with the bourgeois charms of the discrete. HHPA's architecture, whatever its outward "style," is one of combination and assemblage— of collage, of the disposition of "collected" objects. Related to such disparate expressions as constructivism, flower arranging, and the Biedermeier parlor, the force of this way of working comes from a powerful sense of two-dimensional configuring and from an abandoned attitude to juxtaposition of shapes, of materials, of objects, and of styles. Perhaps the most telling example of such a juxtaposition is in the Columbus Occupational Health Center, in which the two most compelling paradigms of glass architecture in the modernist repertoire are boldly bifurcated. An austere, dark, and crisp Miesian box is bisected by a reflectively glazed, mini-Crystal Palace, assembled from off-the-shelf greenhouse parts. The Crystal Palace portion juts out from the building perimeter and is peeled away to form an entrance canopy, irregularly structured to hint at the angled composition within.

This architecture of collage and collection works especially well in situations where a literal collection of something is involved. At the Brooklyn Children's Museum, the difference— purely in terms of "class" of forms— between the architecture and exhibition is indistinct. The corrugated culvert and the flying duct belong to the same family of objects as the plastic molecule model. The Artpark landscape in the landscape conceit is here transformed to the collection for a collection. An equally fine example of the collector's style abetted and abeting an actual collection is the Best Headquarters, designed for clients who not only are leading collectors of the traditional range of modern art objects, but through their patronage have become leading collectors of architecture as well. HHPA's collection of parts and motifs in this building is suave almost to the point of grandeur. It is architecture flowing in seamless consequence of the artistic sensibility of the seventies, a very *modern* building. HHPA here uses industrial parts almost as if they were deco bits. Working within a more generous than usual budget, they have been able to lay on another layer of attention, which yields a textural richness lacking in some of their projects where formal richness is somewhat vitiated by uniformity of texture and surface.

There are two potential problems with this kind of architecture of collection and collage. First, there must be a certain consistency and density of application to avoid being either precious or ironical. These HHPA invariably avoids. The second problem is greater. It is simply that certain juxtapositions do not carry enough conviction to pull the disparate elements together. Both concert halls suffer from this problem. On their outsides, the lumpy brick forms of the auditoriums and the spindly glass lobbies appear infelicitously grafted. Inside, the discontinuities in vocabulary are, if anything, more striking still. This is especially true at Minneapolis where the neofunctionalist lobby is thrown into relief by the essentially traditional auditorium. At Denver the unconventional, "assembled" character of the auditorium is far more of a piece with its lobby, and the two sit better together. The Langworthy townhouse in New York City likewise presents an inappropriate juxtaposition, with an angular modern element sandwiched between upper and lower stories copied directly from 18th-century rowhouses on either side. However, if these are lapses, there is a nobility to them: they are lapses of candor, not of conceit.

RIGHT ANGLES AND WRONG

The discipline in which HHPA's collaging sensibility is at its most satisfying is plan making. If anything, their refined, nonorthogonal plans should be seen as their signature, rather than the blue ducts and pop bric-a-brac with which they are more frequently associated. Like pitched roofs, building plans which deviated from the strictures of the right angle were an early symbol of rebellion against orthodox modernist planning principles. The rotational fever of the sixties was, among other things, an address to the kind of plan which found its culmination in Mies, for whom— as at Crown Hall— the ideal plan was no plan at all. Over the past fourteen years, HHPA has become the undisputed master of the oblique. But what truly distinguishes

HHPA's plans is not simply deviations from the grid but the almost unerring rightness of composition. Perhaps more than any other practitioners currently on the American scene, HHPA has taken a strong interest in the artistic disposition of building elements in plan. At the most purely visual level, these collaged plans are both strong and informal, reminiscent in feeling of the compositional sensibilities that fired the collagings of constructivists like Malevich or Melnikov. This sense of artistic composition is further underlined by the fact that these assembled plans with their discrete forms melded in a gaggle of 15°, 30°, and 45° angles are frequently contained within a simple rectangular building envelope, circumscribing the composition and affirming not only its nonorthogonality but also its two-dimensional origins. These schematic plans look very much like studies for the placement of objects on a stage, to exhaust an analogy.

At a more architectural level, this sort of planning yields a very particular kind of environment, which in HHPA's work falls into several frequently repeated types. If the visual generator is the nonorthogonal composition of simple shapes related to an underlying grid, the main organizing element at the functional level is circulation. A typical HHPA organizational gesture is to throw a circulation axis straight across a building envelope at some appealing and useful angle and then to organize spaces around and in consequence of it. This is done by the insertion of freestanding pavilionlike elements; by the creation of more or less conventional rooms, either at the rotated angle or at the angle of the underlying regular grid; and by the ingenious use of the carefully contrived "leftover" spaces that are created by the collision of the other two elements of organization. To a large degree, projects succeed on the strength of these leftover spaces, which, if not done well, can compromise their usefulness. In general, the strategy seems to work best when the organizational requirements are not too tight, especially in basically open plan situations. The simplest and most elegant example of such a plan is that of the Salisbury School — a square bisected by a circulation spine that just misses coinciding with two opposite corners. At the Brooklyn Children's Museum HHPA elaborates on this bisected square configuration by somewhat greater programmatic complexity and by the extension of the circulation spine to include several levels of activity. At the Columbus Occupational Health Center the spine is greatly expanded, becoming two interlocking L shapes, which describe a square rotated within the large square of the building

envelope and which are expressed externally as shed-roofed, greenhouse forms.

The same motif can be seen in a number of buildings which deviate from the square. At the Mt. Healthy School, for example, a sawtooth configuration allows a series of repeated subdivisions to be placed along a route spine, generating nonregular spaces within and a regular rhythm without. The sawtooth also permits different treatments on the exterior sides of the building, allowing it to shift from effect to effect in response to orientation and to the functions contained. At the Firemen's Training Center HHPA also makes use of a sawtooth plan, but instead of expressing it in the building's elevations, HHPA encloses it in a rectangular envelope, creating a long, high space with a linear exterior wall on one side and a series of zigging and zagging volumes on the other. At the headquarters building for Best Products HHPA uses virtually the same interior *parti* but plays the zig-zag off a gently curving wall of glass block, in what is probably HHPA's most elegant single move to date.

The most diagrammatic example of the use of a circulation route to organize a series of pavilions and places that in turn organize the spaces around them is Artpark. Here the principle is the same as that in the enclosed open plan projects, but the building shell has been left off, exposing the elements. In many ways, this is HHPA's most emblematic work and easily one of their best. The architectural elements literally sit in a landscape, a collagist compendium, like the roof plaza of the Brooklyn Children's Museum, another landscape in the landscape. So clearly is HHPA's work generated by a strong sense of plan composition and interior space, one sometimes has the feeling that the composition of elevations becomes somewhat secondary, wanting the kind of powerful gesture seen in so many of their plans. At Artpark, however, the central circulation element — an elevated timber boardwalk — is truly sculptural, establishing a far more powerful presence than in many of the more mannered projects. Likewise the Best Headquarters is pulled together by a strong and sweeping gesture in the articulation of the facade, induced by its site hard on a major highway. Perhaps the boldest, most unitary form the firm has produced to date is a competition project for an art museum in Los Angeles. This work stands the sawtooth, which so often appears in HHPA's plans, on its side, creating a giant notched-glass slab, which juts dramatically over the street.

Hardy Holzman Pfeiffer's sensibility to the arrangement of

discrete elements within a rigid envelope, visible in so many of their projects built from scratch, has served them especially well in designing the adaptive reuse of older structures. The difference is that, in the older buildings, work proceeds in the opposite direction. Here the envelope into which the new elements are inserted is fixed at the outset, imposing a strong set of demands on what takes place within. It is a discipline to which HHPA responds very well. Since the architectural givens are generally of a strong quality, a dimension that is sometimes missing in HHPA's low-key elevations is provided. This has never led them to dry and impractical archaeology, but rather to a kind of "method" architecture in which they are able to recreate the emotional content of the older work, interpreted through the medium of current methods and materials and in the service of transformed programs. In such projects as the St. Louis Art Museum, the Cooper-Hewitt Museum, and the Willard Hotel, they show a seamless ability to work in the spirit suggested by the original structures.

BETWEEN DREAM AND FUNCTION

Hardy Holzman Pfeiffer's is an architecture of the composite. At its most successful it adduces and celebrates a unity in diversity, a benign pluralism, a cheery coexistence. Theirs is a sensibility that inevitably starts with observation, with picking and choosing. Working at the most catholic limits of eclecticism, HHPA seeks to incorporate the objects of its fancy into built ensembles which both preserve the identities of their parts and forge new wholes. This eminently liberal disposition is thoroughly American in its attempt to reconcile many claims in the service of something larger. For HHPA this larger ambition is not some spurious profundity. Rather it is simply the aim of making places lovely and likeable.

HHPA's sense of the landscape of sources continues to expand. To the early fascination with decorative functionalism have been added successive overlays drawn from both the landscape of the American vernacular and the even larger landscape of architecture's history. But as each new layer of observation is added on, there is no sloughing off the lessons and loves previously learned. The result is an architecture both richer and more relaxed, filled with new possibilities for invention and juxtaposition, balancing a broader and broader constituency of claims. Roland Barthes has described architecture as "dream and function, expression of a utopia and instrument of convenience." Dream and function are happily met in the architecture of Hardy Holzman Pfeiffer Associates.

Projects

Two Offices

In a modest suite of offices for the American Film Institute (AFI) in Washington, D.C., and for a full-blown and lavish corporate headquarters for Best Products in Richmond, Virginia, Hardy Holzman Pfeiffer uses their basic palette of forms and devices to achieve results that differ mainly in magnitude. As in so many of their projects, an enlivened circulation route through a basically rigid, four-square envelope provides the animating gesture for the organization of the interior. At the 1973 AFI the context was some leftover attic at Kennedy Center into which HHPA was charged with inserting offices and a small theater (described elsewhere). As found, the space was "unfinished," that is, finished in a manner HHPA was more than used to exploiting: ducts and piping were already in place, as were concrete block walls. The solution was simplicity itself: first, paint in the designated bright colors of the day; second, lay a slightly kitschy floral carpet along the length of the circulation spine; and finally, erect a series of partitions that cross and frame the circulation route at a 45° angle, lit on one side with a continuous tubular lighting fixture and on the other with a series of large circular ones, which give different character to the space depending on the direction one walks. The angled partitions also disguise the rather grim rectilinearity of the space, creating a humanizing rhythm.

The Best Headquarters — the first phase of which was completed in 1979 — is HHPA's most fully developed and sophisticated project to date, a building which summarizes many of the tastes and tendencies developed over more than a decade. Best is a long building, intended ultimately to be a great semicircle with a curving facade of glass block rising from a moat on one side and with a jagged edge on the other, which maximizes exposures for the individual offices that line it. Inside, the glass block wall stands free, and the second-story floor slab sawtooths along it, creating a series of two-story open spaces, dramatic in themselves and providing visual interconnection between the floors. The round columns that support the slabs are reflected in the round section of the ductwork and in the semicircular air diffusers mounted above the office doors.

Organizationally, circulation is once again the key. A mosaic tile walkway slashes through a sea, or rather pond, of carpet done in a water lily pattern adapted from a silk screen by Jack Beal. Like the building itself, this route curves gently, drawing one through a sequence of openings and past partitions which edge gently up to it, creating eddies of residual space and a sequence of flanking surfaces, many of them hung with works of art from the proprietors' extensive collection. The spirit of collection is pervasive. In this case, the architectural elements are continuous and often indistinguishable from the more purely decorative works of art. The architectural part of the collection includes a system of wooden partitions — deep enough to house desks, shelves, and cabinets — which have elaborately wrought cornices like early 19th-century furniture.

Lighting standards in the parking lot are of a type used in Washington, D.C., in the twenties, and the main entrance to the building is flanked by two enormous deco eagles salvaged from the recently demolished Airlines Terminal Building in New York City. The expression of the principal facade of the building includes a cornice and moulded base, which frame the sweep of glass block, in effect a large-scale version of the wooden partitioning system used within. The facade is an extrusion of this low-key, classically suggestive profile, unvaried over its length. In this respect, it is reminiscent of Cesar Pelli's more dramatic extrusion at the Pacific Design Center in Los Angeles: the definitive profile become building. The difference between the two, however, is in the level of abstraction: Pelli's profile is stripped of its reminiscence of origin. The achievement of the Best building lies in the very sophisticated bivalence in the use of borrowed forms — forms which at once recall their origins and contribute to an overall conception which is completely new.

A pair of enormous deco eagles salvaged from the Airlines Terminal Building in New York flank Best's main entrance.

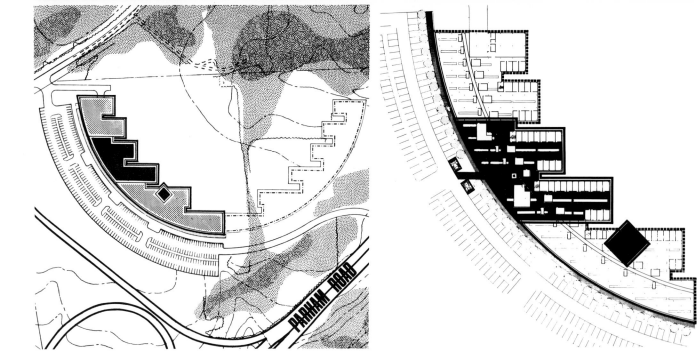

Right: Behind Best's major facade, a zigzagging upper story plan yields a series of double height spaces, interconnecting the two floors.

Opposite page, above: Best's sweeping glass block facade appears as a great bar of light at night, delicately decorated by a diamond pattern in clear glass.

Opposite page, below left: Best's site plan shows construction phasing and the formal relationship of the project to the sweep of the superhighway.

Opposite page, below right: In the first floor plan the mosaic tile walkway parallels the curving facade. Private offices line the edge of the sawtooth.

Left: The collector's approach to the elements of architecture embodied in much of HHPA's work is abetted at Best by the inclusion throughout of a major collection of modern art (shown here in the lobby), spiritually of a piece with the building itself.

Below: Best's gently curving tiled circulation route flows through lily-pad carpet. Partitions edge up obliquely creating eddies of space.

Opposite page: The president's office at Best is simply a collection, the apotheosis of decoration.

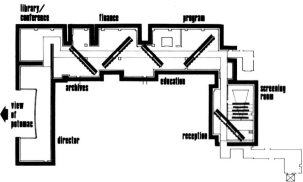

Above and opposite page, above: The American Film Institute offices take on two different characters depending on which way one walks down the florally carpeted route.

Opposite page, below: At the American Film Institute headquarters freestanding partitions cross the circulation route at 45° angles.

Six Theaters

As theater designers HHPA is preeminent. Their work responds to the needs of users on both sides of the footlights by being especially sensitive to the fact that performers and audience *are* in a relationship and that relationship is more than the pictorial, viewer and viewed, relationship of the proscenium. Particularly in the two theaters they have built from scratch, the use of the bare guts, ducts, catwalks, steel rail, and concrete block look throughout establishes a kind of purposeful feeling, a rapport, a collective identity among their users. The first of these projects is the better of the two. The 1968 Robert S. Marx Theater in Cincinnati, Ohio, has a genuinely beautiful plan, and the spareness of its expression is both softened and enriched by its setting in a park, to which it responds both from within, by framing huge views from the lobby, and from without, with the sweeping curve of the auditorium. It may also be the first use of blue airport landing lights in a major project (to fuel a line of speculation). The 1974 Olmsted Theater at Adelphi University on Long Island has an engagingly informal and extremely flexible auditorium designed for teaching drama and has been very well received by its community of users. The exterior is an essay in calculated banality; its style makes it look a lot like a refugee from the little meso-American village at the Firemen's Training Center (discussed elsewhere).

At the 1980 Madison Civic Center in Madison, Wisconsin, HHPA combines old and new, taking a "Moorish" movie theater and a defunct store and transforming them into a cultural complex containing the recycled movie house, gallery space, and a small theater. As always, the restoration aspects are impeccably carried out, completely reviving the fatigued tinsel Topkapi. The whole entity is stitched together with a fine plan, done in neofunctionalist deco plus. The architects outdo themselves in their improbable, but winning, juxtapositions, from the raw cedar and corrugated metal of the little theater, to the oak walls and flying ducts of the "Crossroads," the central circulation area. Again, the elevations are not as stimulating as the interiors: the new-style decoration on the street facade looks pale next to the greater exuberance of the old. The rear is another go at supermarket backside architecture and comes off only within the limits of that self-imposed discipline.

The tiny 1973 American Film Institute movie theater inserted in the Kennedy Center in Washington, D.C., is a delightful throwaway. It sits in its space like a bandwagon or barge and is decorated with automobile parts, an apt metaphor for disposability. The 1969 Exeter Assembly Hall in Exeter, New Hampshire, is another fine melange of old elements and new, an interpretive restoration of real elegance and genuine flash, from its spiffy use of paint, its shiny stainless steel column covers, and the sinuous line of the newly added balcony. The steel underside of this balcony is fasciaed to artfully conceal itself, making it a genuine surprise from where it can be seen. At an opposite pole from the spirit of refinement and precision at Exeter is the New Lafayette Theater in Harlem. Because of its extremely low budget, HHPA responded with what is probably the most "theatrical" of their theater projects and on that level their most successful. Here the entire space is used as if it were a stage, with banks of seats disposed on temporary risers like any other scenographic element, continuous in feeling with the piece that is the stage area. This theater has, unfortunately, now been demolished.

At the Robert S. Marx Theater a strong and interesting form is somewhat diminished in impact by the bleakness of the materials with which it is expressed.

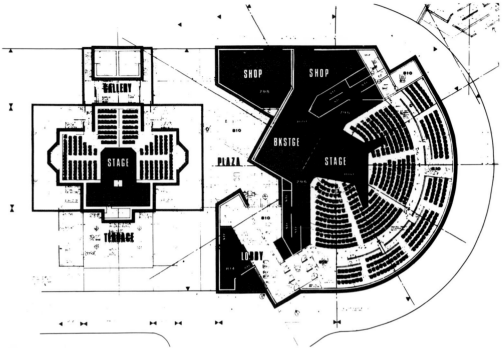

Left: The Marx Theater plan shows the relationship of the large new theater to the smaller one built in an older, existing building.

Below: Forecourt of Marx Theater with landing lights.

Opposite page: There is something vaguely distressing about the single column (with its single protective bollard) which supports the projecting mezzanine of the Marx Theater.

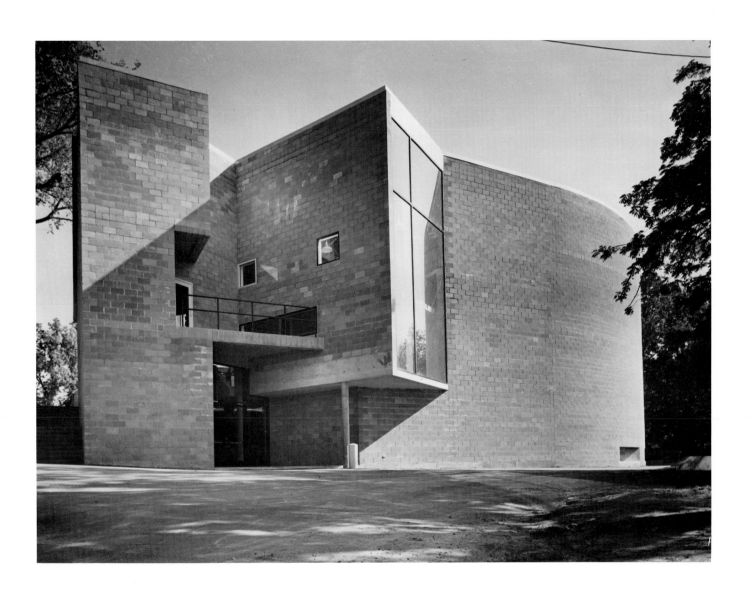

Left: While many of the elements of HHPA's decorative vocabulary appear in the lobby and mezzanine spaces of the Marx Theater, they still have a harshness and austerity which disappear in later projects where shininess is displaced by a growing sense of the lush.

Right: Because there is much more going on, the auditorium of the Marx Theater attains a richness and complexity that dramatically enliven it.

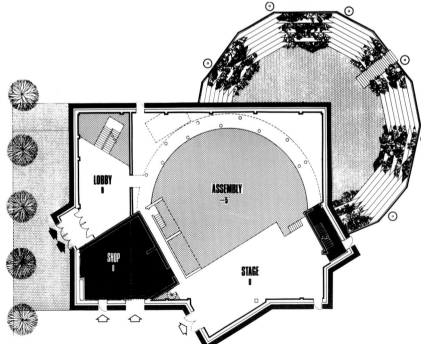

Above: Lobby of the Olmsted Theater.

Above left: Main facade of the Olmsted Theater.

Left: The introduction of circular and rotational geometry within a rectangular envelope creates spatial variety in the Olmsted Theater.

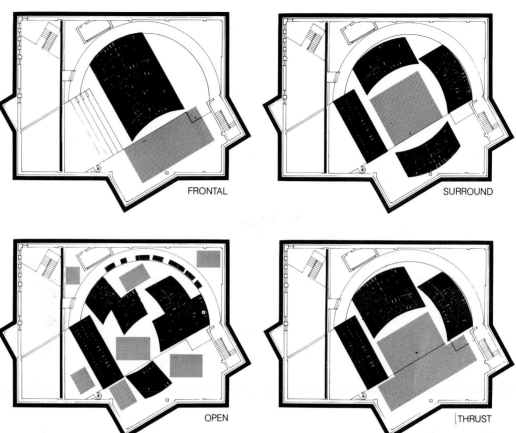

FRONTAL

SURROUND

OPEN

THRUST

Left: As at the Marx Theater, the auditorium is the payoff. Olmsted is a very flexible teaching facility, a kind of miniature total theater which gains great visual force from its down-to-basics approach, allowing the apparatus of play making to speak for itself.

Above: Four basic auditorium configurations can be made at the Olmsted Theater.

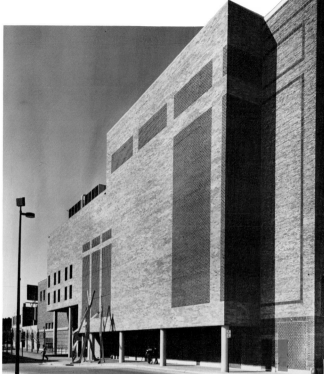

Left: Madison Civic Center's backside architecture.

Below: The Madison Civic Center's central circulation space links the three major programmatic elements and also serves to "absorb" the clash of geometries resulting from the triangular site.

Far left: At the Madison Civic Center new construction is arrayed on either side of the somewhat subdued Moorish tower of a former movie palace.

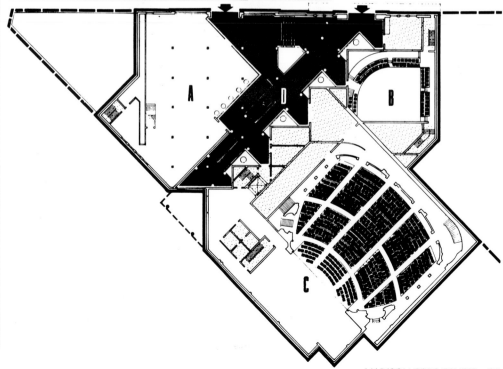

Left: Madison's main lobby and circulation area aims at a deco flavor in such details as the lighting fixtures visible on the back wall.

Opposite page: The original movie theater restored to greater than original glory in the Madison Civic Center.

Right: Grid meets angle at one side of the Art Gallery in the Madison Civic Center.

Opposite page: The most interesting space in the Madison Civic Center is the newly built little theater. Here, in juxtaposing corrugated metal fascias and timber plank walls, HHPA shows the panache that made them famous.

Above and opposite page: HHPA's restoration of this dowdy, ill-proportioned room (above) converted the Exeter Assembly Hall to sleek, yet funky, elegance (opposite page), crossing traditional and modern signals with unreserved verve.

Right: The dotted line on the plan of the Exeter Assembly Hall indicates the outline of the new balcony.

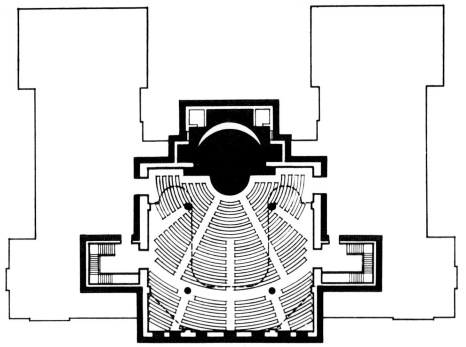

Left: The curving section of the Exeter auditorium is reflected in the curved seating plan, curved balcony, semicircular stage thrust, and the round column covers. Also visible here is a new opening in the ceiling which adds both spaciousness and light.

Opposite page, above: Sections of Exeter Assembly Hall.

Opposite page, below: Until one actually gets under it, the new balcony in the Exeter Assembly Hall looks like it must always have been there. The juncture with the column is a tad clumsy.

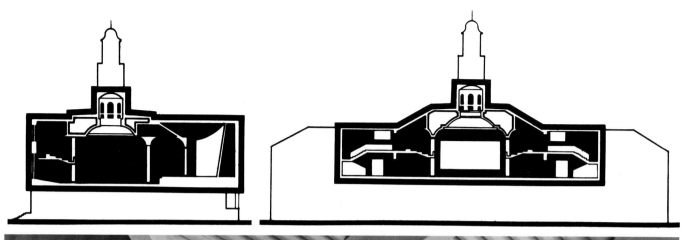

Left: Tucked into a found space, the American Film Institute Theater charms completely. Automobile bits decorate the wall at left.

Below: Plan and section of the American Film Institute Theater, showing the temporary "barge" inserted in an attic room at the Kennedy Center in Washington, D.C.

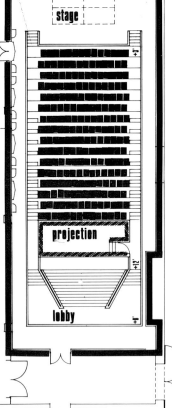

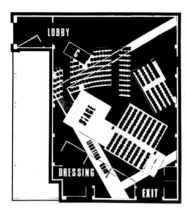

Above: At the New Lafayette Theater, plan as collage, par excellence.

Right: The minimum budget conversion of the New Lafayette Theater makes it in some ways the most theatrical of HHPA's theaters. There is a consistency in the complete temporariness of all the elements, with banks of seats as easily struck as the set, making the disposition of the audience as flexible as that of the lights.

Two Concert Halls

The two projects that have brought HHPA the greatest attention are the concert halls in Minneapolis and Denver. In terms of the concert-goer's bottom line — acoustics — both have been unusually successful. This distinction is the more impressive because the two halls are very different in conception and configuration. Orchestra Hall in Minneapolis of 1974 is based on traditional rectangular precedent — as represented by the Musikvereinsaal in Vienna or Symphony Hall in Boston — with its ancestry updated by principally decorative means. The 1978 Boettcher Concert Hall in Denver, however, springs from more unusual sources. The first "surround" hall in the country, Denver was inspired by Scharoun's Philharmonie Hall in Berlin and the Amsterdam Concertgebouw, virtually the only other examples of this rarely built type.

Because of tight budgets, HHPA elected at both Minneapolis and Denver to concentrate resources on the auditoriums, treating the lobbies and public areas more minimally in ducts-and-girders style. The Minneapolis hall uses the vocabulary of red upholstery, white plaster, and light wood, accented by handsome bespoke brass lighting fixtures on the faces of the balconies. The main decorative move on the interior involves the use of white plaster "cubes" set into the ceiling and cascading down behind the stage. Functionally, these are meant to act as acoustical diffusers. Visually, they are the equivalent of the kind of coffered or putti-bedecked ceilings of older halls, which, of course, had both salubrious acoustical and visual effects. HHPA's cubes work very well at both levels. The sound is superb, and the effect on the eye is striking and original, an effect that works because of the restraint with which the other elements are handled.

The hall appears outwardly to be a great brick lump set at a slight angle in the steel and glass lobby and ancillary facilities that surround and cling to it. While rich use of precedent is used in the design of the concert hall interior, its exterior expression almost completely eschews the kind of symbolism or precedent generally associated with such halls. In terms of its iconography it resembles more the kind of building in which an atomic reactor or recombinant DNA research might be housed: an elaborately sealed laboratory facility at the core surrounded by clean and efficient-looking service space. The rigidity of the distinction between the two parts is partially the result of the "fast-track" method used in construction, which allowed the hall to be begun while the service spaces (which are particularly excellent from the employee point of view) were still being designed. While the building frankly acknowledges the dichotomy between the two, candor may not be exactly the right quality for an environment designed to transport one from the trammels of everyday living to music's heavenly heights.

At Denver the story is essentially the same: a neofunctionalist lobby attached to a dumb 'n ordinary brick box containing a superb auditorium space. While the lobby itself may be less successful than that at Minneapolis, the transition to the auditorium works better. First, the range of colors is consistent throughout, making things feel more continuous. Second, the mood generated by the industrial bric-a-brac and ductwork ganglia is in some way recapitulated by the more fragmented and discrete approach to the assembly of elements in the auditorium. Perhaps because of its unconventional format, HHPA felt comfortable taking greater liberties with the vocabulary of the design, introducing more of the watchmaker's aesthetic of exposed workings. Thus, there is a circular steel catwalk from which lighting is hung and adjusted, itself suspended on cables from the ceiling. Acoustical deflection is provided by a series of shallow translucent fiberglass dishes, also hung from cables, which hover romantically, glowing like a benign fleet of flying saucers. The actual ceiling of the hall, which is flat, is painted in a sort of decorator tartan grid, which some Denverites, appropriately, feel looks like a blanket. This grid, in effect, provides a schematic realization of the relic texture of mechanical systems no longer (for reasons of acoustical isolation) exposed, as well as of the coffered ceilings of the older halls. The massing of the tiers of seats — none more than 95 feet (29 meters) from the stage — is beautifully handled. Overall, a superb, energetic, involving room.

Opposite page: Located at the end of a Kevin Roche—designed arcade which links several elements of a cultural complex, Boettcher Concert Hall—like Orchestra Hall—combines a glassy lobby structure with a brick box housing the auditorium. As at Minneapolis, it works best at night when the colors and rhythms inside are exposed.

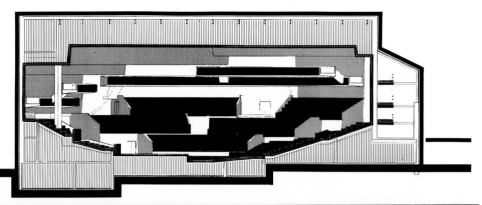

Above and top: In Boettcher's plan and section staggered tiers of seats are assembled in a rich and singular space.

Right and opposite page: Because of the greater risks in its unconventional format, the Denver auditorium scores a greater visual success than Orchestra Hall, abounding with original forms and solutions, all under complete control.

Left: HHPA uses the same essential range of materials in the Denver lobby as in the Minneapolis lobby, but in quite a different configuration. The drooping ducts look like elephants' trunks.

Opposite page: The Orchestra Hall lobby, appropriately, is at its best at night when it is animated by light, color, and movement within.

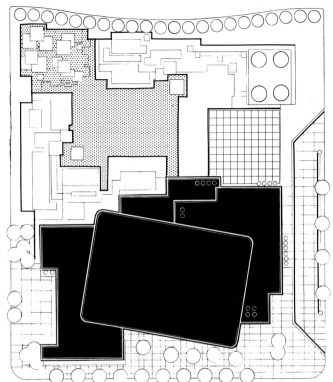

Left: In the Orchestra Hall site plan the auditorium is expressed by a slight rotation.

Below: Orchestra Hall's anti-monumental main lobby facade, in office building curtain wall vernacular, seems overly self-effacing by today's more relaxed standards. The distorted reflection is of the Foshay Building.

Bottom: From right to left, Orchestra Hall's lobby, auditorium, offices, and support facilities.

Opposite page: Elements familiar in much of HHPA's early work—ducts, steel rail, exposed beams—are used in a classicizing, ordered way in the lobby of Orchestra Hall. Here, all the angles are right.

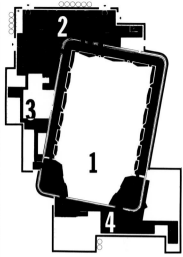

Left and above: Two views of the Minneapolis auditorium. Although based on traditional precedent, the formal means are fresh and very handsome. The space is at once simple without boredom and rich without indulgence.

Above right: Lobby, auditorium, backstage, and administrative components are the four clearly delineated components in the Orchestra Hall plan.

Opposite page, above: Section showing lobby, auditorium, and backstage of Orchestra Hall.

Opposite page, below: The catwalk foyer at Minneapolis is animated by the presence of a crowd, a fine foil to their mutual self-observation.

Below: The music director's office exemplifies the high level of space provided for people for whom Orchestra Hall is a workplace.

Four Educational Buildings

At the Salisbury and Mt. Healthy schools, both of which date from 1972, a similar array of means is used at differing scales. Both achieve great spatial and textural richness within the context of open plans through the use of a careful rotational geometry, skillful organization, well-handled changes in level, and a neofunctionalist imagery that is especially congenial to kids. The highly interactive environments are lucid translations of the open classroom pedagogy of the sixties. The little Salisbury School in Salisbury, Maryland, is disarmingly charming, a contemporary and energetic update of the one-room school house. Its unabashed, yet unpretentious, celebration of simple geometric shapes give it the look of having been built from children's blocks, but perfectly: it is full of casual intensity. The Mt. Healthy School in Columbus, Indiana, conveys the same sense of informality at a larger scale, containing three major teaching "clusters," a kindergarten, and a variety of supporting spaces. In both schools the axial circulation, although clearly the major organizer of the spaces, is actually continuous with the teaching areas, turning it into a useful extension of the "classroom." At Mt. Healthy, elevations are more elaborately expressed, responding to use and orientation and shifting from a highly glazed and somewhat industrial aspect on the cluster side to an extremely long, punctured brick wall on the other two, which, with its coursing and rusticated stone lintels, has an almost Richardsonian flavor, if without that architect's feeling of solidity and mass.

The corrugated metal Firemen's Training Center, built in New York City in 1975, exchanges the whimsy of Salisbury and the outward variety of Mt. Healthy for a more unitary kind of gesture, appropriate not simply to its curriculum but to a dramatic site, which could only be addressed by a move of relatively generous magnitude. The center lies on landfill in the upper reaches of New York's East River, surrounded by water and by a huge and hoary railway viaduct, and sits opposite a mammoth electrical generating plant of truly powerful presence. HHPA's project fits well in this setting: the bermed wedge of the classroom building is dramatic and the descending fenestration pattern at the right scale for the distances at which the building can be most strikingly viewed. Almost equally impressive, however, is a row of "practice" buildings constructed of broadly banded brick and designed to be burned repeatedly. Each is a kind of "everybuilding" — loft, apartment house, factory — and their ensemble forms a kind of dumb 'n ordinary Main Street. The daily conflagration is one of the most succinct pieces of architectural criticism ever rendered.

The inside of the training building, while pleasing in plan with its crisscrossed axes and sawtooth edge, is a bit less successful in built reality. It is harsh in a situation where an atmosphere of calm repose might have been better. Unlike Mt. Healthy or Salisbury the interior is continuous in spirit with the landscape in which it sits: an industrial interior in an industrial landscape. While this has a certain artistic force and intellectual consistency, this was a situation in which a *different* sort of space might have been appropriate.

The just completed Dance Studio & Music Performance Hall at St. Paul's School in Concord, New Hampshire, like the Firemen's Training Center, takes its cues from its context. Here that is the campus of a fine old prep school on a site located between a Gothic Revival building and a sensitively done modern one. Hardy Holzman Pfeiffer has produced a linked pair of buildings that respond to both. The two are placed at right angles to each other on opposite sides of an outdoor circulation route. Otherwise played straight, one end of each building is clad in corrugated metal instead of brick. The conceit is of a building that has been broken in half and rearranged, its raw end just covered temporarily. It works.

At St. Paul's School the Dance Studio & Music Performance Hall's corrugated metal end walls suggest a building sliced and rearranged, a conceit of the temporary.

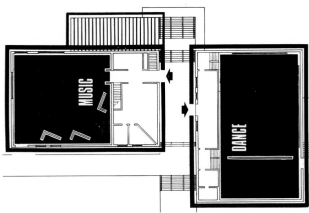

MUSIC

DANCE

Left: The two structures flank a major campus circulation route.

Below: St. Paul's chaste expression blends happily both with the modern building (at right) and with the older academic-Gothic-style buildings which surround.

Opposite page: In the Dance Studio & Music Performance Hall, simple sheds are redeemed by meticulous detail. The shaded sconces in the Music Hall are a particularly limpid touch.

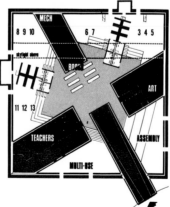

Above and far left: The interior of the Salisbury School provides an impressive variety of space, scale, and sequence with a minimum of means.

Left: In the Salisbury School plan a simple square outside is turned into a group of irregular spaces inside.

Opposite page, above: The Salisbury School's ramped main entry leads intriguingly into a building that almost looks as if it might have been designed by the kids who inhabit it.

Opposite page, below: The rear of the Salisbury School is a little essay into what Hugh Hardy calls the "supermarket backside" style.

Left and opposite page: Examples of the spatial intimacy and richness of detail HHPA is able to achieve with a minimum of means. The module in the Salisbury School is clearly a child-sized one.

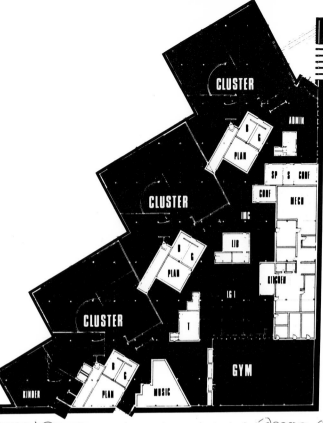

Left: In the Mt. Healthy School plan the three teaching clusters and the kindergarten lie across the circulation spine from common, service, and administrative areas.

Below: Mt. Healthy School site plan.

Opposite page, above: The main entrance of the Mt. Healthy School is flanked by a long "Richardsonian" wall. The wall's apparent massiveness is vitiated—almost parodied—by its actual thinness, revealed as it extends beyond the end of the building.

Opposite page, below: On the cluster side, industrial imagery is softened by an irregularity of application and by functional appropriateness. The shed roof motif and the motif of the projecting brick bays are reflected in the brick wall appliquéd to the opposite side. But the image has shifted: coursing lines and rusticated lintels and coping conjure another 19th-century recollection, the Romanesque revival.

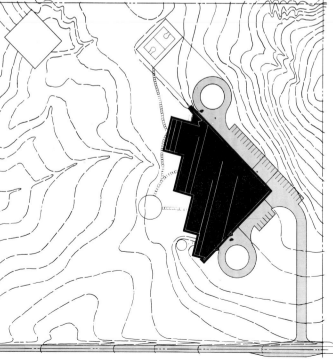

Above left: Familiar kitschy carpet delineates the Mt. Healthy School's main circulation spine over which familiar high-tech elements soar. Partitions, columns, and counterspace abut and intrude with careful familiarity.

Above and opposite page: In the cluster interiors, architectural informality encourages educational flexibility. The open design reflects the open philosophy —serried ranks of desks have no place here.

Above: Seen from the tarmac, the bermed wedge of the main building of the Firemen's Training Center speaks volumes about self-defense. The tank at left is actually a tank. The two which puncture the roof are turrets from which the practice field can be viewed.

Right: An overall view of the Firemen's Training Center site shows architectural gestures effectively scaled to suit a landscape in which nothing is small.

Opposite page: The cluster edge of the Mt. Healthy School enjoys the most favorable orientation and is the most highly fenestrated. Industrial imagery is used at a scale that effectively domesticates it.

Above: Perhaps too much is going on visually in the Firemen's Training Center auditorium.

Right: Mainly regular rooms organized according to a 45° rotation within a rectangular envelope produce a long saw-toothed common area.

Opposite page: On the main corridor, the auditorium is behind the blue-banded volume.

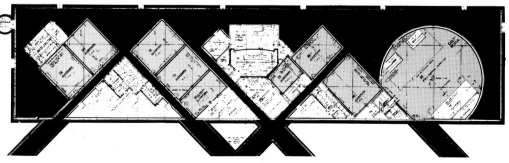

Above and right: Details of ceiling (above) and entry show the elan with which HHPA handles the kit-of-parts palette.

Above: "Main Street" in the little village where trainees practice dousing blazes.

Four Arts Facilities

A hallmark of the architecture of Hardy Holzman Pfeiffer is the degree to which it cooperates comfortably, not only with the objects and collections it is called upon to house, but with the architecture of the past which has so often been called upon to house it. Nowhere are these two affinities more evident than in the renovation the firm carried out on the St. Louis Art Museum, built in the full flush of the Beaux-Arts in 1904 by Cass Gilbert and featuring a main hall done up as the Baths of Caracalla. HHPA's 1977 renovation is refined, respectful, and elegant, the kind of "interpretive restoration" that allows a building to be the best it can by enhancing the qualities of the original. Before HHPA's arrival the museum had fallen into a faded and orderless jumble, the accretions of time working against the spirit of the original, turning a structure of grandeur into a dusty reliquary. Moving in the spirit of the Beaux-Arts, HHPA has made the place once again grand. New axes have been introduced by lining up doorways (with new moulding copied from sources elsewhere in the building), and the original proportions of gallery spaces have been restored. A handsome color schedule has been introduced, and typically sophisticated attention has been paid to relighting, both with carefully controlled natural light and with new artificial fixtures, which, while modern in design, enhance rather than obtrude. A similarly well-executed addition is a staircase leading to a new group of galleries, which, though modern, seem just right.

The problems faced at the Cooper-Hewitt Museum in New York were different. Here the 1976 restoration involved a change of use, and if the building is ultimately less successful as a gallery, part of the reason is that the spaces in the former Carnegie Mansion were less than ideally suited to their new uses. Nevertheless, HHPA's intervention is one of great subtlety and unflagging good taste and shows a degree of self-effacement near flabbergasting in this age of architectural prima donnas and rambunctious intrusion.

Artpark, built on 175 acres overlooking the spectacular Niagara River gorge in Lewiston, New York, in 1974, is a kind of theme park for the arts. During the summer months a variety of resident artists, craftspeople, and performers set up shop on the grounds, and the public passes through and is engaged by the spectacle. Artpark is a virtual diagram of HHPA's compositional sensibilities and devices: outdoors, it presents them with wraps off, pure collage unrestrained by the needs of enclosure. The project is also a map of the landscape of sources that have been prominent in HHPA's work, a compendium of many of the sunnier elements of the American landscape, a collection of images that are incorporated whole and not simply in fragments or reminiscences. The assemblage of boardwalk, barns, silo, brick outhouse (with appliquéd pseudobrick), log cabin, etc., teeters on the brink of a joke, yet is redeemed by its near naiveté, by the appreciative way in which it treats its borrowing, a kind of Disneyland redeemed.

The bermed and buried Brooklyn Children's Museum, completed in 1977 after long development, boasts a compact version of this same landscape on its rooftop. Here the constituent elements include an old subway kiosk, used as an entrance (leading to a huge corrugated tube, which serves as circulation, a subway for kids); a steel silo, which serves as an auditorium within; a couple of enormous interstate highway signs, which announce the museum's presence; and a highway pedestrian bridge, which links the roof to an adjoining park. The basic *parti* is very much like that of the Salisbury School (described elsewhere): a square plan with a major circulation axis, which nearly links two opposite corners. Like Salisbury, this is further elaborated by a series of discrete pavilions for functions that demand enclosure. The museum, however, is a far larger building and includes three separate levels as well as a series of partial level changes on the main floor. Into this varied and lively space — made more so by HHPA's characteristically flaunted structure and mechanicals, never more appropriately used than here — are placed the museum's extensive, largely participatory collections and programs. In spirit, the museum has direct affinities with the philosophy behind the open-plan schools that dominated progressive pedagogy in the sixties. However, the reservations that have sprung up about the absolute viability of that kind of teaching are completely irrelevant here. The Brooklyn Children's Museum is at once a compendium of a child's delights and a storehouse of artifact and information, a structure that truly presents learning as play.

Freed from clutter, the noble proportions of the St. Louis Art Museum reassert themselves.

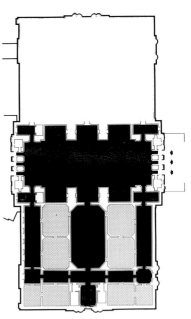

Right: Light from several sources is carefully modulated in the restored gallery spaces in the St. Louis Art Museum.

Opposite page, above left: The sculpture hall in the early twenties.

Opposite page, above right: The sculpture hall before renovation.

Opposite page, below left: A new window, cut from an existing niche in the St. Louis Art Museum.

Opposite page, below right: Lower floor plan of the St. Louis Art Museum.

Above: A sinuous new stair at the St. Louis Art Museum, while unabashedly modern, moves comfortably in the spirit of the original.

Left: One of the new axes opened up by HHPA, spiritually abetting the Beaux-Arts mood.

Above: One of the new axes at the St. Louis Art Museum opened up by HHPA, more Beaux-Arts than even Cass Gilbert.

Left: The dungeonlike quality of the Medieval Gallery was pervasive at St. Louis before renovation.

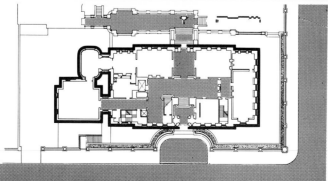

Above: This exhibit room in the Cooper-Hewitt Museum is in the second floor gallery where the original had made no strong mark.

Left: Main floor plan.

Opposite page: HHPA's work turning the former Carnegie Mansion into the Cooper-Hewitt Museum is a near miracle of elegant self-effacement.

Right and opposite page: The main entry and foyer at the Cooper-Hewitt have been left virtually as they were. The only modern intrusion is an elevator which looks like it might well have always been there.

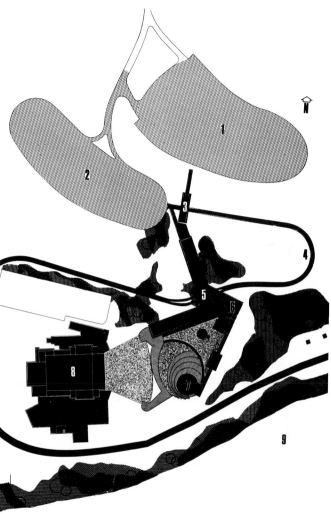

Above: Artpark's site plan is a collage in a landscape. Key: (1) upper parking, (2) lower parking, (3) the "A," (4) walk road, (5) Art El, (6) town square, (7) amphitheater, (8) existing theater, (9) Niagara River.

Left: Artpark's compendium of elements from the naive American landscape includes barns, log cabin, silo, and boardwalk, all elegantly sited in a compelling natural setting.

Above and right: Somewhere between quonset hut and barn, these Artpark structures playfully amalgamate motifs familiar to the American roadside.

Opposite page: The dominating form at Artpark is the elevated walkway which serves both as a visual organizer and as a distributor. Additional elements are located both on and adjacent to the structure, and its elevation permits a stroller to survey both artificial and natural landscapes.

Left: The Brooklyn Children's Museum main display area with circulation culvert and a cheerful weave of building elements. Simple shapes and familiar forms combine with sophistication and verve.

Opposite page, above: A snowy roofscape of the Brooklyn Children's Museum gives only a few hints of the building beneath.

Opposite page, below left: In the rooftop site diagram a typical HHPA zipatone collage represents an architectural one. Key: (1) Entry kiosk, (2) amphitheater, (3) service tubes, (4) silo exit, (5) storage dome, (6) clerestory, (7) sign-light grid, (8) skylight, (9) bridge, (10) exterior exhibit, (11) whale wall, (12) seating.

Opposite page, below right: In the lower floor plan the square is organized by the circulation culvert that cuts across its middle, by changes in level incorporating another geometry, and by a series of pavilions.

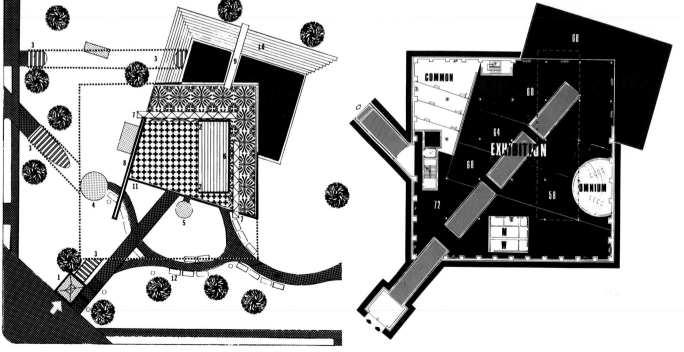

Right: In the Brooklyn Children's Museum circulation culvert, a "stream," part of an exhibit about the workings of waterways, runs down the center.

Opposite page: A remarkable continuity of spirit pervades at the Children's Museum: the visitor's experience is comprehensive, the experience of a single environment and not simply of objects placed within a separate sheltering space.

Two Medical Facilities

Hardy Holzman Pfeiffer's two medical projects, the 1973 Columbus Occupational Health Center in Columbus, Indiana, and the 1978 Eye Institute of the Pennsylvania College of Optometry in Philadelphia, share certain key attributes that enhance their particular strengths. Both occupy parklike suburban settings which suggest a modest scale and order and which enhance the value of openness and long permeable perimeters. Both are low structures, and in both deliberate efforts were made to humanize an environment that is traditionally expressed in a hermetically sealed aesthetic of hygienic terror.

The earlier building at Columbus is the more spatially elaborate of the two, with its meandering circulation route and dramatic interpenetrations, both vertical, past mezzanines and up to skylights, and horizontal, over low partitions and floor-level changes. The Eye Institute is a more conventional two-story building. Organizationally, it bears some resemblance to the Mt. Healthy School: operations are divided into a series of "service modules," which, like the teaching clusters at Mt. Healthy, are both defined and expressed by a sawtooth edge. This edge is wrapped in glass and used as a waiting area, opening onto a view of greenery. The opposite side of the building forms the collective hypotenuse of the sawtooth, although it too is varied with a few modest jogs to mark points at which the row of offices that lines it is broken up to admit light. Within the building is a group of office and examination suites which are rotated against both the perimeter geometries to create a series of irregular spaces around them.

The elements with which the Eye Institute interior is assembled are strikingly similar to those at Columbus. Flying blue ducts abound in both, lime green everywhere asserts itself, striated concrete block forms many of the interior walls, there is plenty of exposed concrete, and fluorescent tubes are used undiffused. In the Philadelphia project, however, this vocabulary is applied with much greater conservatism, yielding spaces which lack something of HHPA's usual zip. Elevations also miss the drama and verve of the Columbus project. The "straight" side is clad in lime green panels, with a strip of large windows surmounted by a row of little ones. The remainder is clad in beige brick, which, on the sawtooth side, is replaced at the three corner jogs by stepping glass sheds, which enclose waiting areas and staircases, like smaller versions of the glass lobbies of the concert halls and which suffer a similar feeling of extraneousness.

Much of HHPA's architecture conveys a feeling of thinness: exterior walls especially seldom offer the sensation of depth, of three-dimensionality. As the Philadelphia clinic pivots from material to material, this sensation becomes acute: the planes are too discrete to convey a satisfying wholeness. With their interior collaging, in which different elements are repeatedly and complexly juxtaposed, the assemblage works, often wonderfully well. In the Philadelphia elevations—like those of the concert halls—the contrasting elements are merely adjacent, and whatever the intellectual or functional rationale, their proximity seems too forced. At Columbus the juxtapositions work because of the continuousness of the materials employed—different glass shapes and opacities—and because of the striking novelty of the geometry and the way in which the different characters of its shifting elevations flow kaleidoscopically one from the next.

Columbus's main entrance canopy reveals and summarizes the building's structural and planning relationships.

Above, left and right: Two interiors of the Occupational Health Center show the familiar range of imagery in HHPA's decorative neofunctionalist style.

Right: The Occupational Health Center has a square plan in which elements respond both to the square's grid and to a rotated geometry introduced by circulation elements.

Opposite page, above: Mirrored shed, dark box, and striated concrete block walls intersect in this rear elevation of the Occupational Health Center, conveying the nonorthogonal relationships of the building's plan.

Opposite page, below: One of the Center's Miesian boxes.

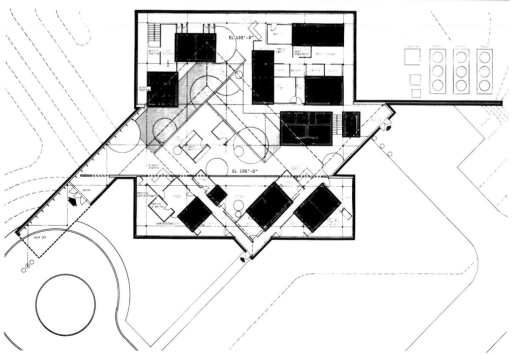

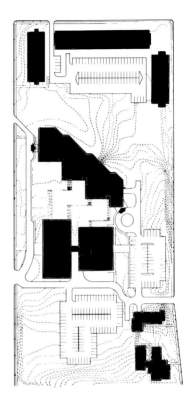

Above: In the Eye Institute site plan a courtyard is created by the relationship of HHPA's building to an existing structure.

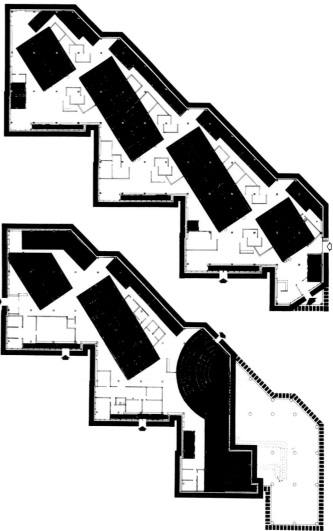

Above: In the Eye Institute upper and lower floor plans three geometries —sawtooth, hypotenuse, and interior cluster — permit the architects to create irregular spaces from regular elements.

Left: As they round a corner, the facade planes of the Eye Institute shift from panel to brick to glass.

Right: A row of examination rooms at the Eye Institute. High-tech forms are more subdued than at Columbus.

Opposite page, above: On the green elevation of the Eye Institute is a jagged array of lime-colored panels.

Opposite page, below: Attached shed forms provide vertical circulation and sunny waiting space.

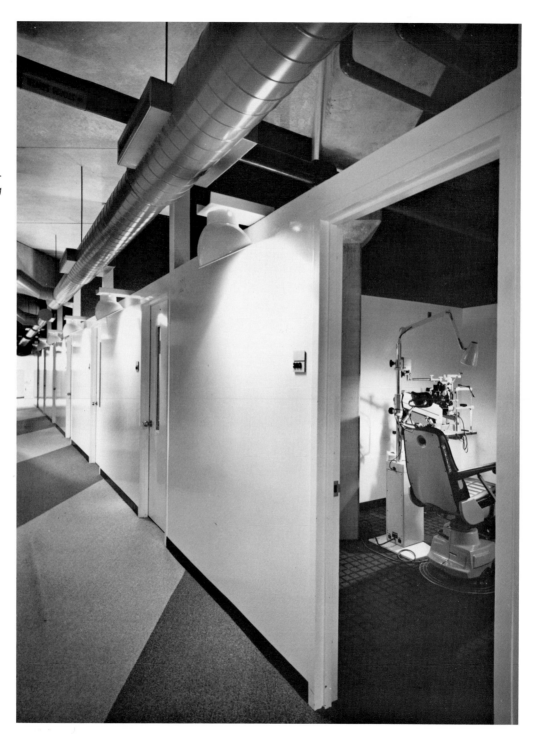

Nine Residential Projects

One could find no better demonstration of the diversity and flexibility of Hardy Holzman Pfeiffer's approach than the houses they have designed over the years. These combine a degree of self-restraint and an adherence to precedent which allows them to be transformed and personalized by the needs and tastes of the inhabitants with enough panache and private character to make them stimulating and special places to live. Nowhere is HHPA's knack for finding the manner for the job more impressive than in these houses.

Designed for a diplomat, the 1966 Dobell House in Ottawa, Canada, is a series of pavilions, articulated by copper minimansards surmounted by a group of mainly south-facing skylights. The house's drama is focused mostly on the living room, a space of considerable complexity in which both natural and artificial light is used with great subtlety to create strong theatrical effects, which change through the course of the day. Equally impressive is the ability of the house to comfortably support the owners' eclectic collection of furniture and works of art. The handling of the poured concrete exterior, while skillful and very much of its time, is not as pleasing, particularly on the less-fenestrated elevations, which suggest Montgomery Schuyler's classic description of the domestic architecture of H.H. Richardson as "defensible only from the military standpoint."

The Hadley House, built in the following year on Martha's Vineyard, shows the clear stamp of the HHPA personality in a work both sophisticated and genial. The plan is comprised of a variety of shapes assembled according to a rotational geometry and arrayed in the service of a spatially complex interior characterized by the interpenetration of spaces and the careful and expressive use of light. The exterior is a funky, assembled collection of shingled sheds, which produces complex shadows and an ever-shifting profile as it is viewed from different directions on its isolated waterside site. There is much wit: from a group of little, one-room, single-pitch guest house sheds located nearby, which look like pieces of the main house that somehow didn't fit in the final assembly, to the shingle-covered flagpole on the big house. The house is unmistakably modern, yet responsive both to the conditions and atmosphere of its site and to a venerable tradition of shingle style building.

Two adjacent houses occupying former storefronts in Boston are succinct samples of HHPA's knack for rotational configuring within the regular constraints of a rectangular envelope. The

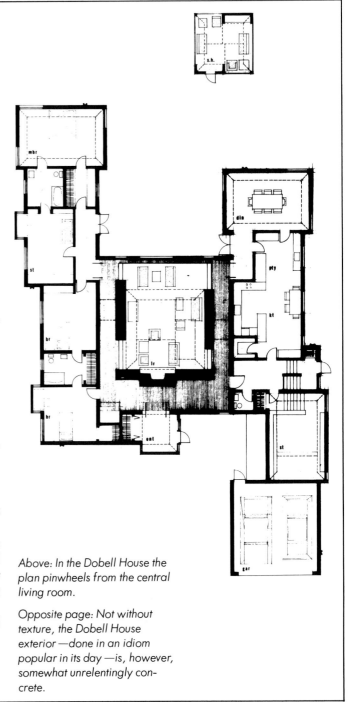

Above: In the Dobell House the plan pinwheels from the central living room.

Opposite page: Not without texture, the Dobell House exterior —done in an idiom popular in its day —is, however, somewhat unrelentingly concrete.

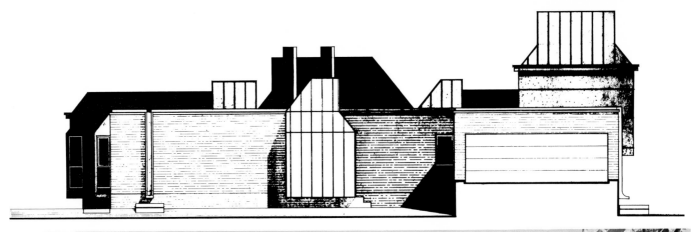

Opposite page, above: Dobell elevation.

Opposite page, below: A group of "light-grabbers" help to break down the scale and impart rhythm to the profile of the Dobell House.

Below: Theatrical lighting effects and a carefully modeled ceiling give presence to the Dobell living room. Hardy's first house finds him undaunted by the need to design in concert with an eclectic collection of objects.

Above: One of HHPA's most beautiful ceilings provides a strong gesture which calms the almost frenetic visual activity of this Hadley House bedroom.

Right: A trademark duct sprouts like a fiddlehead fern.

Opposite page, above and below left: Responding to the hoary tradition of shingle style beach houses, the Hadley House transcends in its amiability. Its outward complexity is purposeful, expressive, and fun, deflating the seriousness of the genre with such winning moves as its large circular balcony, its shingled flagpole, and cheery anemometer.

Opposite page, below right: The rotation pivots on a central fireplace.

project—the 1968 Avery Johnson House—comes off with particular success because of the simplicity of both means and program and because of the instinctive way in which the architects handle the introduction of natural light and the elaboration of circulation, which is both complex and efficient. A similar plan strategy was used in the 1979 Langworthy House in New York City. In this instance the construction is entirely new, although the party wall/rowhouse situation is essentially the same. Here the expression of the off-grid interior pattern on the street facade is unsuccessful in its context, giving away what comes as a delightful surprise in the Johnson House.

The Knowlton House, built in 1969 in Sneden's Landing, New York, follows a pattern in many ways similar to those in the Johnson and Langworthy houses, but here the house is freestanding. A large and a small rectangle are linked by an entry area, and a secondary grid is introduced at 30° to the long axis of the plan. Spatial variety within results both from spaces, which penetrate both levels, and from a complexly pitched roof, which interacts with the angles in the plan to create various faceted spaces, all of which gains richness from the overlay of domestic artifacts. In the 1970 Cloisters Condominium a series of shed forms is used both to establish the identity of individual units and to give the project as a whole the feeling of townscape, an urbanized version of the Sea Ranch spirit. Built on an "impossible" site overlooking the Ohio River in Cincinnati, the complex has only two basic plan types, essentially rectangular, but given variety by triangular bay windows, off-grid interior balconies, the roof pitch, and window shapes which respond to it. The real texture of the project comes from its ensemble, its rhythmical stepping down the hillside, the timber poles and angled bracing that support it, the lively exterior circulation, the sweeping views, and its jagged and picturesque hill town profile. Perhaps the most engaging, however, of HHPA's roof forms is that of a little pavilioned link between two existing waterside cabins for the Duncan family in the Adirondacks. Here the beams, exposed pitches, and irregular shapes are used with casual purpose, gracefully joining the original cabins and moving fully in their spirit and in that of the landscape.

At the 1974 von Bernuth House in Dobbs Ferry, New York, HHPA was designing for a client with an extensive collection of 18th- and 19th-century English and American antiques, yet who wanted a decidedly modern house. HHPA's design suits these requirements admirably, achieving a spatial variety and providing a contemporary environment in which antiques sit comfortably. The plan is an A shape, with public areas at the apex and entry between the two legs. A series of small changes of level on the main floor are made possible by artful siting on a mild slope, and these, along with a lightwell formed in the rotated square at the apex of the A and a group of cabinet/partitions orthogonally related to its cross-piece, generate a complicated and pleasingly ambiguous sequence. As always, light is cagily modulated and materials juxtaposed (steel structure, wood beams, and clapboards on the interior) with an artfully studied freedom. The exterior is less impressive but seems to aim at underwhelming, its brown shingle cladding melting self-effacingly into the woodsy surroundings.

A more architecturally scaled juxtaposition of old and new is to be found in the 1974 Pratt House in Bridgewater, Connecticut. The architects have added onto a former barn (originally converted to a house in the 1920s) by, in effect, running a rectangular form at 45° through the middle of the existing barn, creating a sort of horizontal version of the juxtaposition made vertically at the Langworthy House. Here the results are more pleasing. On the exterior—where the new element pops out in a series of rotated cubes—the whole building seems very much of a piece, the contrasting geometries far happier when unconstrained by the need to fill in a row of houses with established and strong character. Inside, HHPA shows their usual adeptness in using rotational geometry to organize space and sequence, as well as their accustomed dexterity at juxtaposing texture and style to achieve a laid-back harmony in diversity.

Right: Finished surfaces introduced in a rotational arrangement play successfully off the rough brick of the original shell in the Avery Johnson House.

Below: The plan and section of the Avery Johnson House show HHPA's characteristic geometry inserted in an existing storefront.

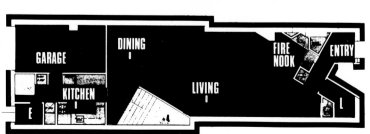

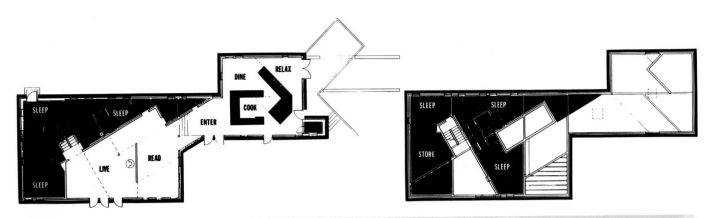

Opposite page, above: In the Knowlton House plans a large and small rectangle are linked by a small square which carries a secondary geometry derived from the line which joins the upper right and lower left corners of the plan.

Above, above right, and opposite page, below: New additions to the Knowlton House are both frankly acknowledged and immediately familiar as they pass through and attach themselves to the existing structure. The knitting together is greatly enhanced by the controlled casualness with which everything is joined.

Right: Sited romantically on a Cincinnati hillside, the Cloisters Condominium is at once evocative of Italian hill towns and of the vernacular of gathered sheds that were then sweeping the profession behind the leadership of Charles Moore. Although large relative to the scale of its immediate surroundings, the project appears to be a completely natural outgrowth of the existing fabric.

Below right: At the Cloisters Condominium romance is imparted by supporting large projecting balconies on poles, adding an extra bit of precipitousness to an already dramatic setting.

Below: This relatively simple plan configuration is given subtlety and richness by the way in which it responds to the steeply sloping site.

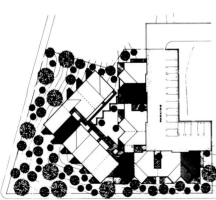

Above and right: HHPA's project for the Duncan Compound links two existing cottages with a new kitvhen and dining area, which, although clearly new, continues the spirit of its predecessors. The slightly cumbersome exterior is amply validated by the scintillating forms within which perfectly frame a letter-perfect landscape. Note the period supergraphics, in whose use HHPA was a pioneer.

Left: The simple shingled exterior of the von Bernuth House with its large single-paned windows is both modern and unobtrusive in its woodsy context. Hints of a more complicated sensibility can be glimpsed through the front door where a balcony is seen in midflight and an unexpected paper covers the walls.

Top: Section of the von Bernuth House.

Above: The von Bernuth House has an A-shaped plan with circulation organized along the crosspiece, which also serves to separate public and private zones.

Above and right: In the von Bernuth House a sublimely eclectic interior happily houses the owners' extensive collection of antiques. The symmetry of the plan is reflected by the two facing chairs (and ten facing pictures) which sit on a little balcony at the apex of the A. Lighting is particularly fine, as is the conceit of the casement in the clapboard gable, which seems to suggest that the inside is out.

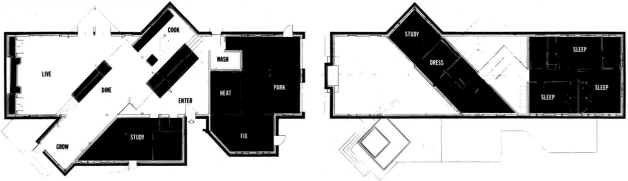

Opposite page, above: New elements pirouette out of the existing structure of the Pratt House like benign growths.

Opposite page, below left and right: The new elements at the Pratt House —conceptually two bars of space —are slipped in above and at right angles to each other on a grid at 45° to the existing main axis. One side of the upper bar has been trimmed to conform to the roof profile, while the opposite simply pops out.

Above: The original house was demolished in an accidental explosion that killed several members of the Weather Underground. If the new Langworthy House calls perhaps too much attention to itself at the expense of the unity of the historic row, it effectively marks an important, if unacknowledged, monument in American history.

Chronology

The nature of this volume precludes appropriate mention of all the people whose aesthetic, technical, and administrative talents have informed buildings in the following list. They are a splendid and talented crew who deserve full recognition. By way of compromise we have at least credited those at work in the office during 1981.

Hardy Holzman Pfeiffer Associates

HHPA STAFF

Partners:
Hugh Hardy, FAIA
Malcolm Holzman, FAIA
Norman Pfeiffer, FAIA

Associates:
Alec W. Gibson, RA
Victor Gong, RA
Kurt Kucsma, RA

Architectural:
Eric Anderson
Richard Ayotte
Curtis Bales
Ann Benson
Carol Berens, RA
Donald Billinkoff
Diane Blum
Susan Butcher
Anthony DeSimone
James DeSpirito
Neil Dixon, RA
Violeta Dumlao
Maurice Farinas, RA
Harris Feinn, RA
Jaime Fournier
Theron Grinage
David Gross
John Harris, RA
David Hoggatt
Tony Hsiao
Alfred Katz, RA
Don Lasker, RA

Thomas Little, RA
Pamela Loeffelman
Hilda Lowenberg, RA
Raoul Lowenberg, RA
John Lowery
Leah Madrid
Jack Martin
Carol Maryan
Jerry McDonnell, RA
Mike McGlone
Thomas J. McNamara, Jr.
David Mohney
Lynn Redding
Stephen Saitas
Todd Sklar
David Stein, RA
Abby Suckle
Craig Swanson, RA
Claudio Veliz
Sergio Zori, RA

Administrative:
Louisa Chan
Robin Gale
Theodore Grunewald
Clare Hamill
Betty Lau
Beth Mollins
Cleo Phillips
Karen Ross
Sherry Rosso
Kathleen Thompson
G. Scott Walsh

1963

Playhouse in the Park: Phase I
Cincinnati, Ohio

1965

Playhouse in the Park: Phase II
Cincinnati, Ohio

1966

Simon's Rock Art Center
Great Barrington, Massachusetts

Performing Arts Center
University of Toledo
Toledo, Ohio
(Not built)

Ingersoll Residence
Sharon, Connecticut
(with T. M. Prentice, Jr.)

Dobell Residence
Ottawa, Canada

1967

Hadley House
Martha's Vineyard, Massachusetts

1968

Robert S. Marx Theater
Playhouse in the Park: Phase III
Cincinnati, Ohio

Johnson Residence
Boston, Massachusetts

MUSE
Brooklyn, New York

New Lafayette Theater
New York, New York

1969

Exeter Assembly Hall
Phillips Exeter Academy
Exeter, New Hampshire

Taylor Theater
Lockport, New York

Knowlton Residence
Sneden's Landing, New York

Duncan Compound
Adirondacks, New York

Newark Community Center of the Arts
Newark, New Jersey

1970

Cloisters Condominium
Cincinnati, Ohio

Exeter Theater
Phillips Exeter Academy
Exeter, New Hampshire

Shaw Master Plan
Shaw University
Raleigh, North Carolina

Community Services Center
Shaw University
Raleigh, North Carolina

1971

Tufts Theater
Tufts University
Medford Massachusetts
(with Earl R. Flansburgh and Associates, Inc.)
(Not built)

NCSA Master Plan
North Carolina School of the Arts
Winston-Salem, North Carolina

Dance Theater of Harlem School
New York, New York

1972

Cultural Ethnic Center
New York, New York

Salisbury School
Salisbury, Maryland

Mt. Healthy School
Columbus, Indiana

Emelin Theater
Mamaroneck, New York

Webber Ski House
Stratton, Vermont

Spaeth House
Easthampton, New York

1973

American Film Institute Theater & Headquarters
Kennedy Center
Washington, D.C.

Columbus Occupational Health Center
Columbus, Indiana

1974

Artpark
Lewiston, New York

Orchestra Hall
Minneapolis, Minnesota
(with Hammel Green & Abrahamson, Inc.)

Olmsted Theater
Adelphi University
Garden City, New York

von Bernuth Residence
Dobbs Ferry, New York

Pratt Residence
Bridgewater, Connecticut

1975

Firemen's Training Center
New York, New York

Agnes deMille Theater
North Carolina School of the Arts
Winston-Salem, North Carolina
(with Newman VanEtten Winfree Associates)

School for the Creative and Performing Arts
Cincinnati Union Terminal
Cincinnati, Ohio
(Not built)

1976

Cooper-Hewitt Museum
New York, New York

Terry Dintenfass Gallery
New York, New York

Hartford Square
Hartford, Connecticut
(Not built)

Baskerville Hall & Wingate Gymnasium
City College of New York
New York, New York
(with S. W. Brown & Associates)

1977

Brooklyn Children's Museum
Brooklyn, New York

Eliot Feld Ballet Studio & Headquarters
New York, New York

St. Louis Art Museum
St. Louis, Missouri

Bridgemarket
New York, New York
(Not yet built)

1978

Boettcher Concert Hall
Denver, Colorado

The Eye Institute
Pennsylvania College of Optometry
Philadelphia, Pennsylvania

1979

Langworthy Residence
New York, New York

Southwest Hangar, Miller Field
Gateway National Recreation Area
New York/New Jersey

Best Products Corporate Headquarters: Phase I
Richmond, Virginia

1980

Dance Studio & Music Performance Hall
Experimental Theater
St. Paul's School
Concord, New Hampshire

Museum of Contemporary Art
Bunker Hill Competition
Los Angeles, California
(Not built)

Madison Civic Center
Madison, Wisconsin

Spirit Square Art Center
Charlotte, North Carolina

A SELECTION OF CURRENT PROJECTS

American Film Institute/West
(Adaptive reuse/Rehabilitation of existing campus)
Los Angeles, California

Ballet Theatre Corporation
Rehearsal Studio & Offices
(New construction within existing structure)
New York, New York

Best Products Corporate Headquarters: Phase II
(New construction)
Richmond, Virginia

Brooklyn Academy of Music
(Rehabilitation)
Brooklyn, New York

Con Edison/Queens Division Office
Con Edison/110th Street
(New construction within existing structure)
New York, New York

The Currier Gallery of Art
(Rehabilitation/New construction)
Manchester, New Hampshire

Elgin Theater
(Rehabilitation)
New York, New York

Eugene Performing Arts Center
Eugene Parking Facility
(New construction)
Eugene, Oregon

Grand Central Terminal
(Exterior restoration)
New York, New York

1894 Grand Opera House & Hotel
(Rehabilitation/New construction)
Galveston, Texas

Market Square
(Urban revitalization)
Pittsburgh, Pennsylvania

National Recording Studios
National Theater Center
(New construction within existing structure)
West Side Airlines Terminal
New York, New York

The Pingry School Campus
(New construction)
Bernards Township, New Jersey

Russell Library
(Rehabilitation/New construction)
Middletown, New York

Sloss Furnace Cultural Center
(Rehabilitation/New construction)
Birmingham, Alabama

Symes Townhouse
(Rockefeller guest house restoration)
New York, New York

Virginia Museum of Fine Arts
(Addition/New construction)
Richmond, Virginia

Willard Hotel
(Restoration/New construction)
Washington, D.C.

PHOTOGRAPHY CREDITS

Unless noted below, photographs are the work of Norman McGrath or from the files of Hardy Holzman Pfeiffer Associates.

30, above; 86–87; 88, above and below right: Neil Dixon
40, above: Herndon Associates
63, 64: John Veltri
77; 78, below; 79; 80; 81, 117: Cervin Robinson
78, above right; 81, below: Richard Benkof
88, below left; 89: David Hirsch